WITHDRAWN
UTSA LIBRARIES

THE
CANAL BED

Also by Helena Minton:
  After Curfew in *Personal Effects*
  Alice James Books, 1976

THE
CANAL BED

———————————————

poems by

HELENA MINTON

ALICE JAMES BOOKS

Copyright © 1985 by Helena Minton

All rights reserved.
Printed in the United States of America.

Book design by Susan Graham
Typesetting and paste-up by Type for U, Cambridge, Mass.
Photographs by David DeInnocentis

The publication of this book was made possible with support from the
National Endowment for the Arts, Washington, D.C., and from the
Massachusetts Council on the Arts and Humanities, a state agency
whose funds are recommended by the Governor and appropriated by
the State Legislature.

Library of Congress Catalogue Card Number 84–072463
ISBN 0–914086–52–9 (hardbound)
ISBN 0–914086–53–7 (paperback)

Alice James Books are published by
the Alice James Poetry Cooperative, Inc.

Alice James Books
138 Mt. Auburn Street
Cambridge, Massachusetts 02138

LIBRARY
The University of Texas
At San Antonio

ACKNOWLEDGMENTS

Grateful acknowledgment is made to the editors of the following periodicals, in which these poems, often in different versions, first appeared:

The Beloit Poetry Journal ("Persephone," "The Hunt," "On the Tundra," "Maps," "Taboo," "From the Same Cloth"); *Chomo Uri* ("Visit with My Mother"); *The Colorado State Review* ("The Abandoned Mill"); *The Connecticut Poetry Review* ("The Field by the Tew-Mac Airport"); *Dark Horse* ("In the Underworld"); *Green House* ("The Roses"); *The Harbor Review* ("Dogs Named After Islands"); *Images* ("Two Views of Plymouth"); *Karamu* ("Sitka Spruce"); *Loom* ("The Canal Bed"); *Outerbridge* ("Until It Ends"); *permafrost* ("Legend"); *Poetry* ("Artifacts," "Bread," "Letter"); *Sojourner* ("Ghosts in the Garden"); *West Branch* ("Presences," "When I Get Up in the Morning I Don't Know Who I Am," "Minus Tide," "The Locket," "Housekeeping," "Ninth Month," "Burning the House").

Several of these poems also appeared in a pamphlet, *In Another Life,* published by Watch City Press.

The quoted material in "The Canal Bed" is taken from *The Old Middlesex Canal,* by Mary Stetson Clarke, The Hilltop Press, 1974.

I wish to thank Mrs. Eleanor Torrey West, of the Ossabaw Island Foundation, where some of these poems began. Thanks also to the Arts Council of Wilmington, Massachusetts, for a small grant, which enabled me to work on this collection.

And I would like to thank Hilary Douglass Horton for her impeccable editing; all the poets whose invaluable criticism helped shape these poems; Barbara and Ed Monkiewicz for the summer on Shuyak Island; and Bink Noll, David and Marion Stocking, and Chad Walsh for their encouragement and support over the years.

CONTENTS

ON THE TUNDRA

TABOO

GHOSTS IN THE GARDEN

ALWAYS BY WATER

For My Mother and Father

For David and Ted

ON THE TUNDRA

Shuyak Island, Alaska

THE HUNT

I touch the pelt nailed to the wall,
black tail, black stripe along the spine.
I want to pull it over my shoulders
and walk out, bare feet burning
on the icy streets.

                    After you shot the buck
you had to shoo away three deer,
which sat beside it.
Wind blew toward your face.
You left the head in the moss,
eyes black and glassy.

Last night I went back for the skull,
picked clean in tundra snow.
It spoke but soil absorbed its words.
What I held was your head,
hollowed in tundra air.
I knew I would leave my body
next to yours.

              Turning in sleep
I saw the deer stand up again,
sheathed in sunlight as you shouted.
Lifting their heads in the wind
they blinked, their eyes not quite believing.

PREPARE

To lend tea bags, halibut hooks,
your dry floor to a stranger.

To work with hands
that break out in welts,
spend weeks without
books or butter.

In December
when the man you live with
takes the skiff to town,
he may not be back.

Hang the deer in a tree.
Keep the lamps lit.
Carry your rifle everywhere.

ON THE TUNDRA

We saw the sow and her cub
running along the cliff,
away from the sound of the outboard,
and slept badly, thinking of the gun
that jammed, the wife who had to shoot
to save her husband,
the crewman who came back from a walk,
his left eye bleeding, right arm bitten off.
But we needed food,
carried our rifles across grass
worn through by years of paws.
On the path lay pebbles
bears shit out months ago,
eating an otter or seal.

Wind stripped us down
to our walking scent,
strong as the ocean's,
a texture to our flesh
only the bears' teeth could know.
I imagined them watching,
eyes powerful as our scopes.
Ahead, the cliff, cormorants
shrieking up and down its face.
We hiked all afternoon.
Deer trails stopped without warning
in clumps of spruce, as if
at the end of a long walk
the animals turned into trees.

ARTIFACTS

Wind blows from the mainland across the Straits,
over nettle-covered middens where we've dug
for Aleut arrowheads, unearthing
fishbones, clam shells, human teeth.

Tribes slept near these hills
and in daylight told of omens dreamed
as salmon, startled elk.

Trout broach, eagles circle
yet never enter my sleep.
I thought out here the mind would empty
and be filled as quietly as sky with stars.

When I close my eyes I see torn sheets and blackboards.
I want the spruce, sea otter, cormorant
inside of me to speak.

16

SITKA SPRUCE

Blacker than water, branches churn,
blades in a hard wind,
timber so dark I want to
peel back the bark, expose
the white meat of wood,

or follow the ways of old tribes
that weakened trees with fire.
Flames smoldered around a trunk
for weeks as they chipped away with stones.
One log held forty whale hunters
clutching their spears.

Without tools, with no idea
how to turn a forest into oars,
I walk the beach gathering deadfall.
Trees blanched by tidal waves
lie on their sides, roots thrust in air.
I break off branches and carry what I can.

FOR BRADLEY SARGEANT

You rationed daylight like water,
chopped wood, greased otter traps,
and mended nets, the bone needle
big as a child's crayon.
As you sat inside, slow, by the fire,
fleshing hides, you talked to yourself,
worried images from a past you couldn't change.
Or else your mind went blank,
a stone on the outer beach.

What did you look forward to?
Nets squirming with salmon?
Caribou in your sights?
Or a full bottle of whiskey
floating in off a freighter,
a naked woman stepping out of a canoe.

You bent to your axe, your nets and traps,
until the wind wore through.

PRESENCES

I walk through the wind to the garden,
thinking of Sargeant salting salmon
on this portage forty years ago.

Peas bloom in the ruins of his smokehouse,
nourished by his ghost —
a quiet spirit, I've decided,

who sold his fish in silence,
glad when the last canoe pulled out.
I talk to him

       which I can't do
with the people in our cabin,
blown in for days from Blue Fox.

They eat our food, use my hairbrush,
dry their faces on our towels,
fill the room with cigarette smoke

and when I reappear they laugh,
surprised, forgetting
who I am.

VESSEL

Its rim is crusted with salt
from scaling fish,

blood when you rinse
your hands after hunting.

Its base curves like a shield.

I carry it to the clothesline
tucked at my waist

and the crook of my arm,
a posture so natural

I might have held it
in another life.

20

BREAD

Dough rises in the sun,
history of the human race inside it:
orgies, famine, Christianity,
eras when a man could have his arm
chopped off for stealing half a loaf.
I punch it down, knead the dark
flour into the light, let it bake,
then set it on the table beside the knife,
learning the power
cooks have over others, the pleasure
of saying *eat*.

LETTER

To Alice Cronan Minton

I liked to sit at your dressing table.
Whiskey-colored perfumes smelled of dust.
The photograph beside the mirror showed
a serious face, a man in *pince-nez,*
who died the year I was born.

Nights, lying on the fold-out couch,
I was surrounded: mahogany, Chinese lamps,
and paintings of forests
boxed in by big gold frames.
Nature felt confining,
closing in as you grew old.

This summer I sleep on a barge,
stare at spruce and sky
as I walk this island, which hasn't changed
since our Celtic ancestors invaded Ireland.

1909 you were twenty-two.
I picture you in Boston
practicing piano scales
the day Mount Augustine—the volcano
I see from the beach—spilled lava into the sea.

Perhaps you saw it in the paper, perhaps not,
concerned with music or men or money,
gold-rimmed plates and goblets of your future.
If you thought of any other world
it was Europe, Strauss waltzes,
a honeymoon tour before the war.

LEGEND

No one has spoken for two days.
On our marine band, static,
faint Japanese, the same foreign noises
ringing in wind, in water.

After a storm flotsam litters the stones
like debris from a party:

the bourbon bottle,
gold calligraphy on its label,
may have floated from Kyoto;

this black boot slipped
off a fisherman's foot.

The braided rope held a crate
or was wound into a noose by hands
that changed their mind.

I take the cup back to the cabin,
a blue cup, a horse etched on its side.

Pour nothing in.
Out of it will spill
the voice of the last one who drank.

MINUS TIDE

I often feel we're here to reconcile,
though we haven't been apart,
but lived for years like an old couple,
their children grown, most of their lives
behind them.

          Think of them on this island
during a minus tide, picking their way
past bladder wrack and jellyfish
to test the ocean. Are we different?
Mornings we row to the nets,
find our herring smeared with algae,
and spend the day wanting to be consoled,
holding a book in the hammock or the grass,
wind blowing the same paragraph past our eyes.

When it rains we're outside
weighed down by rain gear,
or in the cabin playing gin,
withdrawn behind the fan of our cards
into layers more molten than the earth.
If our hands touch, reaching for the deck,
we pull away, startled.

A ship churns deep in the Shelikof.
I wish I were with the fishermen
approaching port, hearing shouts at dock.
We make the only human sounds,
but small, smaller than the bees',
whose noise is twice their weight.

THE MOUNTAINS OF TEN THOUSAND SMOKES

When I row I feel them closing in.
Through fog they're wisps,
barely visible, photographs of the soul.
If the sun sends down its spokes
peaks rear from the ocean,
hard white folds disgorging mist.

They shift their weight
when I blink, as if they might
rise up or sink and take me with them.

The boat floats forward, its prow
like two hands pressed together.

TABOO

Ossabaw Island, Georgia

TABOO

*. . . any wrong deed committed by
the expectant mother will injure the
unborn child. She must not walk
alone, sit alone, dance alone. . . .*

Margaret Mead
Coming of Age in Samoa

I'd like to think our house is made of grass:
we coax the baby out with food,
beat my belly with a stick;
I squat and he falls
onto a pile of leaves.

But he floats inside his salty tank,
no larger than the hermit crabs
racing across the beach.
Some are being born as I stand here.
Lizards breed along the banks.
Petals drop from the magnolia's
egg-shaped blossoms.

You are far up the coast among maples.
Do you hammer Sheetrock, preparing his room?
I study the Spanish moss like a picture
in which your face is hidden,
looking for an eye, a cheekbone.
In a dream a stranger fathers the child.

I lie awake, the mother of twins,
the one inside me, the other
I stopped from growing ten years back.
Windows open onto a terrace
where people talk into the night

about the Civil War, failed orange crops,
black women dying in childbirth,
taking with them infants
who only breathed an hour.
Their bones lie under snake skins
in neglected cane fields.

If you were here we'd follow
roads through cabbage palms,
brushing past tung trees and wisteria,
walking carefully, knowing everywhere
we stepped might be a grave.

BURNING THE HOUSE

Five bricks remain:
French windows, white pillars, a view of Spanish moss.
Think of the woman who furnished it:
Every day the island took her husband up.
He saw to rice fields and plotted orange groves.
His crops were carried down canals
that lay like full-length mirrors in the wilderness.

Pregnant, she dreamed of childhood's
pink interiors, clean as a conch,
her fingers falling on the keys
as the piano echoed her uneasiness,
always out of tune in the heat.

She waited for the midwife,
swatting gnats, her motions
slow as a sea turtle
settling its belly in the sand.

She burned the house down
in her mind so many times
that when the Yankee soldiers
lit the sheets, she felt she'd struck the match.
Flames roared through her closets.

Hiding with her family
like deer in the reeds,
she watched the balconies collapse
and all the beams, fire shooting toward the water
as war freed her from the island.

WHATEVER IS INSIDE

A family came here each spring
to breathe camellias
while the king snakes slept.

I tiptoe through their rooms,
peer in mirrors, pick up keys,
as if this were my grandparents'

pink stucco house and I a child
playing hide and seek,
waiting hours to be found.

Where the carpet ends
things echo, cooks bang pots
and laughter spirals up the back stairs.

Sheets soak in soapstone tubs,
one black woman up to her elbows
in suds, another slamming down an iron.

The laughter stops when I enter.

———•✦•———

Our family used to dress for dinner:
Emil in bow tie, white hair slicked back like feathers,
Kathleen, hands folded before the meal,
looking out over the family as over a garden.

And the cousins, silent, in smocked dresses,
ears opening like petals:
a girl   expecting   too soon

And Kathleen, pushing back her chair:
What will it matter in a hundred years?

———•✦•———

Her grandmother made chicken sandwiches and set two
eggs in a pot. The child stood by the stove, watching
the eggs bubble and click, touch without breaking.
Her grandmother put the sandwiches and eggs in a basket
with raspberries and lemonade and drove to the golf course,
where the grass stretched, one lawn after another with
no house. The club arced through the air like a whip.
The child washed balls in the scrubber, felt the
brushes whir against the pockmarks. Then they sat
down in the gazebo and opened the basket. She
tapped the egg on her knee, looking out at the gray
clouds pressed low over the trees, until she felt
something ooze down her leg, a mass, gelatinous,
the uncooked white. "Whoops!" her grandmother said,
whisked the egg into wax paper, handed the child a
raspberry. As she brought the berry to her mouth she
saw little red bristles like chin hairs sticking out
of each red nub and dropped the berry down between the
slats of the bench onto the grass, which lay clean
as her grandmother's rugs. All afternoon she held
a golf ball, glad whatever was inside would not get out.

————•+•————

Kathleen, I didn't think to ask
what it was like to be pregnant.

Did you feel as I do now,
unable to put one word after the other,

as if you were buried and couldn't get up,
shaking away any hand?

Did you feel shame among strangers?
Like the cow that chews sitting down

meaning it will rain,
more an omen than a human being?

I can't imagine your screams,
the sweat of your hair on the pillow,

only your voice, its sharp Canadian *R*'s,
which once taught schoolchildren how to count.

How did you feel knowing bones
were growing inside you, muscle and heart?

I give myself the advice
you would if you were alive: *Sleep   Eat well*

NINTH MONTH

Ten years ago on Vashon
around a house half burned by vandals,
blackberries grew so thick
I cut a path to the door.

Friends cleared a hillside,
planted food to feed a town,
and left, tired of each other.

I used to stare across the Sound
to the lights of West Seattle
and imagine a father who watered the lawn,

petals dripping in headlights,
a mother who paused on the stairs
to hear her children sleep.

Tonight as we wait, I lean by the window
as if on that island,
watching for friends who never came back.

What house do you remember?
What faces gathered at the table?

You put your hand on my belly,
surprised by its hardness.
The child who grows inside will ask
for stories from us both.

GHOSTS IN THE GARDEN

THE BLOODSTONE

Once as a child on a plane
I wandered down the aisle until a man's hand
stopped me: Did I want to see his ring?
The gold rose like another knuckle
cupping a green stone
streaked Christmas red.

His sandpaper breath scratched my neck
as he pointed past the wing
to mountains, saying the stone
had formed there, deep under the snow,
boiling and flowing, hot and rising
to the top of the earth to harden.

He rapped the ring on the pane,
making a fist, veins puffing
along the back of his hand,
black hairs twisted up his wrist
into a sleeve stretched
stiff as a bed sheet.

Each time I flew I saw his hand
shaped in a cloud, his ring
a stab of sunlight on the window,
listened for his whisper
in the air vent,
until I was afraid to fly.

I stayed on the ground
like a sinner in the Middle Ages.
But still the red crept in
through stained glass, apothecary jars,
the lining in an old man's coat,
as he lifted his whiskey to the light.

WHEN I GET UP IN THE MORNING
I DON'T KNOW WHO I AM

If I were a child
I'd play street hockey.

But I might be the mother
making her wear mittens

or the mother's mother
knitting the mittens

or the father telling his wife
to buy food for the blizzard

or the neighbor
wishing she knew the father.

If I were the paper boy
I'd be up at dawn.

The mother would feel
too tired to sweep.

If I were the father
I'd think of the neighbor
climbing her stairs alone.

The mother's mother—
who'd think of me
setting the table at noon?

If I were the blanket
I'd be folded back,
smoothed by the neighbor's hands.

If I were the child
I'd wonder why Mother
stood smoking at the open door,
snowflakes in her face

as if expecting Father,
who won't be home for hours.

GHOSTS IN THE GARDEN

Last winter we walked through the supermarket,
slush on our boots,
shocked by the price of melon.

You remembered luncheons
your mother gave in Seattle:
honeydew, prosciutto, strawberries.
You left as soon as you were twenty.

The summer I stayed with her
I stood on the lawn while she hosed down
her rhododendrons.
We sat on the porch,
wisteria blowing around us.
She played gin with my grandfather.

On visits East they stayed at the Waldorf.
We went out to dinner, the theater,
my grandmother in cool black furs, jewels,
smelling of lemon blossom.

Back home you brooded in our garden,
tossed cigarette butts in the flower beds.

This evening I arrive for dinner.
Her china shines on your table.
Azalea and aster envelop the yard.
The sprinkler turns through sunlight
as though a hand with diamonds on it
flashed across the lawn.

VISIT WITH MY MOTHER

I see you less often now. Teatime,
a tray placed on the polished table,
windows turning blue with dusk,
smell of sweet peas, even in winter.

You bend to pour the tea.
Steam drifts up.
Your face is smooth as marble.
You wear your mother's ruby on your hand.

As always, I admire your objects:
violets pressed in glass, pale vases,
miniature angels playing violins,
bulls in oils, silent, obedient,
the way you chose them.

While we talk you break dead leaves
off a chrysanthemum,
adjust gold cushions
as if arranging a still life.

We discuss our work,
facing each other
in blue armchairs, women
the same height and weight
wearing wool and silk.

THE ROSES

In the late afternoon,
wearing gloves, my mother
bends to pour bone meal
on the flower beds
until every inch
of earth is white.
Each year more roses
surround her house.

Last August I was sick.
She brought me the Mojave,
her prize rose.
When the wind blew
petals drifted
on my wrists, across the sheets,
curled and dry
as insect husks.

Every winter my father hands her
roses, awkwardly unburdening
himself. And she accepts,
placing the stilt-like stems
in water by the window.
Against the bald sky
those dark formal flowers
unfold.

HOUSEKEEPING

The woman down the street
hangs out her clothes like paintings:
Monet's violet-flowered sheets,
the Grant Wood of her husband's jeans,
tiny T-shirts and pink socks: Paul Klee.

They smell of sunlight when she reels them in,
folds back sleeves like wings
and smooths the sheets shyly
as if touching her husband.

Outside, leaves keep falling.
They cover her yard, so many,
such odd shapes, if only
she had drawers for them
or could mail them out like bills.

Everywhere underground lie
bulbs she buried at random,
like balled-up socks in a drawer,
forgotten under the dark snow,
until the crocuses surprise,
objects she thought she'd lost:
combs, mirrors, cups, brilliant
spools unwinding.

PERSEPHONE

My mother is still beautiful.
Her hair has the sheen
of an oak struck
by lightning.

The field hands will do
anything for her.
They gather the sheaves,
grapes, olives, all
she asks. They heap
the harvest in her lap.
They do mule's work
to please her.

She says it is because
of the light I cast,
the pigment I put
in the leaves that shade them
after work. And yet
I am only a shadow
dragging after her.

White hills and houses
hurt my eyes.
The sea sends up
its slime, its jellied hands.
I stay indoors and wait
until I can replace
the iridescent greens
with grays and browns.

46

My mother falls asleep.
Her fields dry up.
I go back underground,
lungs black as a miner's,
my husband, a shadow,
holding out his hand.

THE LOCKET

We did not paint each other
nude in the forest.
My face did not dissolve
between your hands
as we had written.

We were going to run away
not to Brazil but Indiana:
we imagined the swimming hole,
the diner where we'd drink our coffee,
cows rubbing noses by the fence,

and recorded it on onionskin,
a pact we set on fire, swearing secrecy,
storing the ashes in my locket.
We closed the curtains and lay down
hoping never to get up again.

Today the locket broke, fell open like a gate
in a gust of wind, ashes blowing
toward the house we pictured,
the crumbled chimney, cobwebbed rooms
where no one would want to live but us.

TWO VIEWS OF PLYMOUTH

Last week at the museum
I pressed a button and a light went on
in Myles Standish's house.
Cabbages shone by his door.
Women knelt in the fields;
around them a fence
enclosed the diamond-shaped fort
built from green felt.
Each inch of village held a story:
a birth, betrayals, quarrels
between the twig-like couple by the road.

On a brief flight out of Boston
I see the same town without boundaries:
schoolhouse, factories, cranberry bogs
sprawled along the ocean.
A figure walks against the surf.
I think this is a man I loved
grown small as the child we lost.
His shadow stripes the water,
white sand smoothed around him
as though he is fixed there,
waving, while only the plane moves away.

UNTIL IT ENDS

1.
This is the season people leave each other,
as if we weren't lonely enough.
We need to find new territory.
Some night you'll head west on I-80
until it ends
in redwoods and eucalyptus,
the relief of new smells
and silence of coastal towns
where no one knows your habits.

2.
I wanted to stay forever in Blooming Grove, Ohio.
Leaves blew in the deserted bandstand.
A woman leaned out a window
like a cuckoo clock
but the boy on the bicycle
would not come home;
the lady on the porch
would not complete her knitting;
the men in the tavern
would never finish their beer.
It was as though they expected
to be kissed awake,
as though the town had been created
to disappear in.

THE INSTITUTIONS ON OUR BLOCK

for Nora and Sean Minton

Who knows what's worshiped in this temple?
Two nights a week men file in
leaving wives and children behind.
They wear suits and ties.
They mumble secret chants about brotherhood,
Masons, sharpening tools
more mysterious than the mortician

next door, enveloped in wisteria.
He hides his clean, black limousines,
leaves two lamps on all night,
curtains parted, shadows cast
as in a dim boudoir.

Up on the hill the hospital hums
with life-support systems:
X rays, brain scans, probes
that tell the sex of the baby
or the size of the cyst,
enough morphine locked in its cupboards
to put this town to sleep.

I still tell the seasons
by staring at grade-school windows.
Today thirty turkeys are pasted to the glass.
The panes wait for snowflakes and hearts.
Planets hang in the main hall,

a luminous mobile, Pluto
and Saturn's pale-yellow rings.
Maps of the world are nailed to the doors,
rivers flowing in red ink.

At three o'clock, children walk out
of the building, up the street,
wearing black pointed hats
and feathered headdresses,
their lips buzzing with new facts.

ALWAYS BY WATER

THE CANAL BED

*Built in 1793, the Middlesex Canal
ran from Lowell to Charlestown,
Massachusetts.*

The canal has been abandoned
and found again
by antiquarians
walking the side roads
up to their knees in leaves.
Some sections still fill
with water, others lie
buried under roads.

You grew up here.
When the guidebook says it passed
through the softball diamond at Foss Park,
under Boston Avenue Bridge,
between Wedge and Winter duck ponds,
you see traffic lights,
graffiti scrawled above the railroad tracks.

I trace its course along the map,
picturing scenes from old engravings:
boats loaded with coal,
Baptists immersing themselves,
skaters circling bonfires,
and Woburn, where the first Baldwin apple
was grafted by the colonel
who ran the canal
until the railroad wiped it out.

Picnickers rode packet boats
to the Lake of the Woods:
"The sun set, the moon rose,
the band played
and gentlemen sang songs."

———•+•———

You snap your wrist,
the line flies out.
You lean the pole
against a rock and wait,

part of the twilight.
I stand beside you
watching for rainbow trout
to rise in silver rings.

We do not speak or touch,
our eyes drawn
to the surface the sun
fills with purple as it sinks

half in, half out of water.

———•+•———

It took eight hundred hours
to build the boat by hand,
gray with black shutters,
moored by the old Baldwin house
on a half-mile stretch of water.

Sundays they offer rides.
The day we went, the horse,
stung by a bee, bolted back
across the highway
through the shopping center
to the barn.

Our wide flat street
is part of the old towpath.
At night I imagine water
flowing beside us, hooves,
cargo hauled to Boston.

Instead, dazed teenagers dare
each other: they knock down
trash cans, stone walls,
hide in the shrubs
until the police leave.

———•╪•———

Honeysuckle shrouds the canal
at Thorndike Street in Lowell,
but straight ahead roll
the Merrimack's broad waters.

No place to sail.
We'd have to stop at the dam,
portage through the parking lot
of Archambault's funeral parlor.

Better to stand on the bridge,
stare at rocks slippery
with moss or over our shoulders
where the river widens
and at dusk turns an oily rose.

A door bangs in my sleep.
I should set it on the water
like a raft.

How far could I go
before I ran aground,
reached Black Brook Lock,
no one in the tollhouse to open it?

———•+•———

This is the way excursions end:
railroad tracks stop in a field,
the road curves into someone's yard.

What can we do but get out and walk,
leave the canoe,
carry the camera and picnic basket,

straggle through twilight arguing
who misread the map,
took the wrong turn,

or else sit down in a field,
eat the remains of lunch,
pretend we are waiting for help,
pretend help never comes.

———•+•———

Always by water—
the Concord, Shawsheen,
Aberjona,

small pools,
or the Atlantic's
violent wake—

walking by water
brings us close.

Here are photographs we took
last year in Wilmington
in the ruins of an aqueduct.

Gray clouds drifted
between the trees
like ghostly undersides of boats.

Wild grapevines grazed our heads.
Roots burst from stone.

THE RIVERBANK

When you see a speck in the sky
you cry *bird*.
You haven't learned *swallow* or *crow*.
A stalk of ryegrass
you call *flower*.

What you drink from your cup,
what falls from the sky,
what flows past us now is *water*.
You don't know *river, rain,* or *tear,*
or the *rough gray-green* reflected beside us.

Trust me when I say we're surrounded
by *air*. It carries *baby* and *backpack*,
but the word you hear me sing
so often, *love*, seems spoken
by a mother in a book
leaning to another child.
Hand feels truer. *Branch.* *Stone.*

To you the word is one more sound.
You point to the setter across the river
as if you could touch him.
I'm holding you when I say
love. Do you hear me, far away?

DOGS NAMED AFTER ISLANDS

When we call our dogs we are honoring
volcanoes, the continental drift,
God's casual hand in creation.

They race towards us like boats,
steering between islands,
a wake of insects and weeds.

We call back places
we'd like to settle in
but never will,

a windy Alaska portage,
a shack on Puget Sound,
our boots rattling gray stones
shaped like totems:

Shuyak   Vashon

Strangers struggle with the syllables,
humoring us, as if we had named
our children after trees.

Asleep, they curl like islands
seen from the air.

Often, thinking of something else,
we touch them as if
trailing our hands in water.

THE FIELD BY THE TEW-MAC AIRPORT

Mornings I walk through foxtail
to a weed-filled runway, head down,
thoughts scattered like milkweed.
The dog crashes through cattails,
flushes mourning doves.
He sniffs, stops, points
as if in a painting.
Above us small planes test the air's mood.

Yesterday someone screamed, ''Are you crazy?''
I turned to see a green wing
almost touching my shoulder, a fist
thrust from a cockpit; then I heard
what I should have earlier: wheels
skittering like bird legs on asphalt.

I ran to the pines, watched the plane
lift shakily into the wind,
the pilot's fury spread through the sky,
while I pressed my cheek
against the dog's cold neck.

FROM THE SAME CLOTH

for the mill girls,
Lowell, Massachusetts, circa 1840

The city fathers dreamed these girls
the way they dreamed the town:
to scale, pale colors on a map, dolls
bending at looms by day, reading
the classics by night. Now I imagine them
as they rise to bells, break ice
in washing bowls, file at dawn
to the mills, their breath pouring before them.

All day they stand, each girl
at a different task: to guide raw
cotton through the spindle, blend dye
for yellow calico, count each bolt
for dish towels, sheets, their future husbands'
shirts, their own petticoats.
They hear machines roar the way the river
roars, breast wheels turning.

Do they whisper sonnets to themselves
or think of Cleopatra on the Nile,
clay banks where men lie sleeping?
Do they dream of being loved like that?

Each time a girl writes home, part of her
follows the letter across the border
to New Hampshire, growing damp
as it passes the sea, then safe,
unfolded by her mother's hands.

When she places her cheek on cold cotton
she sees the years ahead
like yards of undyed linen,
and yearns to watch a warehouse full
of dimity catch fire.
She wants to walk past the row
of beds, down to the river's most
seductive bend, to lie on the grass,
wet blades staining her nightgown,
feeling the hush, the sound
of nothing being made.

THE ABANDONED MILL

To a woman driving by at night
the mill seems more like home
than the houses she passes,
their cheerful army of lamps
inviting yet sending her away.

She remembers how she walked here
as a child, her hands stretched out, in shadow.
She came because she might get hurt
or lost so far, her friends
would never find her, stepping into a mirror
and never coming back.

She breathed the spidery smell,
found the best corners
for an echo, shouting as she
wanted to in church,
rubbing the floor's worn hollows.

Tonight, beside black walls, black
windows, black sky, black water,
she lets the darkest part of her lie down.

BY THE MERRIMACK

I walk a path built of granite,
wooden rail at the level of my hand.
I want to follow the entire river
as it flows through names
I've seen on maps: Manchester, Concord,
city of peace, of smooth, fat grapes,
and the villages: Tilton, Riverhill.
I'd pass each in one stride
until I reached the first
drop of water as it fell.

I could continue to the corner
where New Hampshire narrows,
darkens, its houses sparse,
and this river's sister,
the Connecticut, begins.

Or I could walk the other way.
No one knows where the river
ends, the ocean starts.
As a child I tried to pinpoint the spot,
believing I could find a seam,
a line of sunlight on the current
between fresh water and salt.

It's like the place one falls
in and out of love: now sharp,
now sweet, the wrists
plunged in, the same
steady pressure of longing or regret.

DRIVING HOME FROM WORK

Route 38, Lowell

Wet headlights slide past.
Each car bears a driver to a different house.
"Come home with me," I say to shadows racing by,
as if they were spirits who had risen from the river,
not faces I see in the supermarket.

The drivers want to enter a stranger's house.
Those who usually stay up late
will fall asleep by the fire,
while the rest of us sit drinking
rum from teacups, talking about our lives.

No one is waiting for us at home.
They have all grown up.
They have fallen in love with others.

Apples gleam on the sideboard.
Someone stirs, unbruised, on a mattress.
The sun does not rise
until we are ready for it.

IN THE UNDERWORLD

I wonder if he has considered what I might be like
down here, underwater, buckets
lowered past my shoulders by girls
doing daily chores. Later
their lovers row them on the lake.
Boats move over me
the way his body used to,
a flick of oar in greenish sunlight.
Then the couples who braided
their bodies together
betray each other.
He lies in the woods with someone else.
She cuts her wrists, recovers.
Down here I watch the water
freeze and melt,
trees stare at themselves.
A hiker stops to rest.
He might be Orpheus,
his memories of me distorted
like a face in rippled water.
I remember how his shoulder heaved
as he turned back to look,
and then the lake
closed over.

MAPS

We haven't been anywhere in years,
so we open the atlas, pausing
over cities we might walk through.
Brushing the pages, you say,
think of a map for the blind,
skin would get wet
when it felt the Mississippi,
or cold on the Matterhorn.

My hand twitches over the continent
as if it were a Ouija board, landing
in a country of white stucco,
lemon trees, convents
converted to hotels.
I remember each guest slept
in a chamber once meant for penitence.
Who thought of the accumulation
of sins, those bare knees on the floor?
Not I, lying beside a man who's stayed for years,

a memory below my skin
like a country under tracing paper.
I touched him where the sun darkened his arm,
running my fingers down the lines
in his left palm through his future,
looking for myself.

I haven't told you that part of my life,
the first half, filled with foreign names
and the belief that I could always go

on other journeys, that my mistakes were correctable,
like the cartographer's spelling.

I lean across the couch to whisper to you.
You sleep, your head thrown back
looking old, so old I think
you might have lied about your age
until I see the yellowed atlas,
its outdated boundaries of half the world,
and realize how much time has passed.
I close my eyes to touch you.